Speak into Your Own Life:

Thirty-Day
Prophetic and Inspirational Devotional

To Purpose

Margaret G. Green

Edited by Lisa Thompson at writebylisa.com.

Paperback ISBN-13: 978-1493767076

Ebook ISBN-10: 1493767070

Table of Contents

Introduction

Words are powerful! They can change your behavior and ultimately shift your whole life.

Proverbs 18:21 (NIV) says, "The tongue has the power of life and death, and those who love it will eat its fruit."

"'For I know the plans I have for you,' declares the Lord, 'plans to prosper you and not to harm you, plans to give you hope and a future'" (Jeremiah 29:11, NIV).

How do you learn your purpose? Yes, we all might have had or currently have this question. Today I want to challenge you to find out what you were called to do. What has God placed on the inside of you, that special thing that causes your heart to beat, that gives you life, that you could do whether or not you were paid because it's just in you to do? Yes, that thing. And if nothing came to mind, I want to challenge you to pray for divine revelation of what that is. God will answer you.

And because you have a purpose, it's time to start speaking to it! Get ready to make room. Where you currently are (your present circumstance) does not fit where you're going.

Listen, it's never too late to seek your purpose and God's will for your life. If the Lord told you everything that you would face, you might give up. So instead he prompts you to focus on him. I touch and agree with you that before the year is out, you will have a certainty and a surety on who God has called you to be and on what he has called you to do. No more wondering, inconsistencies, guessing, second-guessing, or operating below, outside, and beneath the capacity in which you have been called. Be encouraged—this is the last year you will go through this. Fear will lie about the outcome of your situation. It's not that God didn't say it. Fear stepped in and said you couldn't do it! I loose it off you now in Jesus's name. Now proceed forward! You don't wait to live. You make an intentional decision to live. Where you are now looks nothing like where you will be tomorrow. I know that some of you reading this might feel like you missed your opportunity to do the will of God, but late does not mean you missed it. The Lord just wants you to start—start speaking so that you can start doing and achieving. Listen, your areas of testing are most likely your purpose and what you were created to do. You can never miss God; he is way too big for that, but you can miss your purpose if you focus on the small things.

Your biggest challenge in life will always be you and the greatest person you could ever be is you. There will never be another you. You are what has set you apart from them. After you have overcome all the negatives, faults, in capabilities, and what you perceive is unsuccessful or unattractive concerning you, you will be able to see the man or woman that God has created you to be! It's okay; embrace and love yourself. Be happy with yourself, with all of you, because Jesus is. You might not totally understand your purpose. This might be a constant question as you become more aware of Jesus Christ and who he is, the reason why the Lord has allowed you live through so many things and the reason you wake up every day. There just has to be more, right? Well, yes, there is. Do you really think that he allowed you to go through all of that just to exist? No. A thousand times no. He wants you to live, truly live. I encourage you today to stop for a few moments and simply ask the Lord what your purpose is and watch him begin to unveil what he's called you to do. He's already been trying to show some of you. If you would just stop and take in the scene around you. Expect a return on your investments.

You will get out much more than you put in. When you invest in the Lord and in his kingdom, wow! The return is off the chain!

In this process to purpose, don't lose sight of who you are and what you are called to do. The trials in this season are directly connected to your destiny.

We are not our struggles, neither are we what we struggle with, but we are the finished product of what the Lord has called us to be. Don't beat yourself up; you'll get there. You will make mistakes; it's impossible not to. I'm just saying.

The drive keeps the dream alive. If you really want it, go and get it. It's yours for the taking. Popularity does not guarantee success, but the favor of God allows it. Believe God for the unexpected! Be blessed. Continue to pray and ask God to reveal your purpose. More than likely, the Lord is trying to show you something.

Don't waste time staying upset over missed opportunities. Look forward to the new opportunities to come, like the one that's knocking at your door right now.

Pep talk before your breakthrough to purpose.

Think about who or what wants to stop you.

Answer: The trials of life, stress, the enemy, discouragement, fear, finances, yourself, and other people, depending on how big your purpose is.

Decide who and what will stop you. Answer: nothing and

nobody!

Pay close attention to the following. There is absolutely no such thing as perfect, but there is such a thing as willing. If you are willing, you are ready to be used in whatever capacity the Lord wants to use you, regardless of the opinions of others. I can't wait to see how the Lord uses you. Promise me, yourself, and whatever you were created to do, that no matter what you do in this season, no matter how hard it gets, no matter how much you struggle, you will not close your mouth. You will not lose focus but will continue to persevere, push through, and speak life over yourself, your spouse, your relationship, your business, your career, your education, and what the Lord has given you to do. We need you to survive, my sister and my brother.

DAY 1

Listen, the rest of your story has already been written. Psalm 139:16 (NIV) says, "Your eyes saw my unformed body: all the days ordained for me were written in your book before one of them came to be."

We don't always make the right decisions, according to the will of God. Let that not be the reason you stop pressing on. I know it doesn't feel good to disappoint the Lord, but he just wants you to get back on track. Walk in the newness of life and continue to listen the voice of the Lord. He will never lead you astray. Remember, humble beginnings move you into big endings. Despite what happened or how things have turned out thus far, I was sent to remind you that this is your season. This is your time. It is your turn—I repeat—it is your time. The setback was a set up for an explosive miracle. I recall having so much zeal for what I wanted to do, submitting so many different ideas, but having them rejected to the point it almost killed my confidence. But, the Lord encouraged me to keep going because it either wasn't time, or it just wasn't a fit. So his words were DON'T GIVE UP…CONTINUE TO SEE IT THROUGH!

The great thing is, you don't have to do a lot at once. Sometimes doing too much at once can hinder the vision. Don't worry, you don't have to do it all today! Believe God for tomorrow, and let tomorrow take care of itself. Take a well-deserved break when needed and come back to it. I promise that you will be able to think more clearly. I know it's just the first day, but starting with a clear mind and a clean slate is essential to getting on track.

Remember that anyone who is irrelevant to the vision has no power over the outcome of the vision. Their verbal assent means nothing. Trust the Lord; all will be well.

The Lord said, "Rejection killed your confidence, but my glory and anointing shall revive and restore the confidence that you need in this season in order to fulfill the promise.

Get ready. The Lord said, Although they said no, I'm saying YES! They may not like you, they may even not understand you, but they cannot deny what I've placed on the inside of you!

Don't allow your situation to hold you back from your dreams. Who lied and told you that you couldn't do it because you had kids or because you didn't go to school or because you don't know the right people? Remember that you can do anything you put Christ to. What better way to show that God can do all things.

You don't have to have an answer to every question. The Lord wants you to take the time to think and meditate on it a little longer. Sometimes the Lord will allow you to downgrade just so that he can upgrade you to something better than before.

If you change your attitude, you can change your atmosphere. If you change your mind, you can change your future. If you change your relationship, you can change your marital status. If you change your friends, you can change your drama to peace. And if you change the way you live, you change who you see and where you go when you leave this life. Make a change today for Jesus Christ. A change for Purpose.

The hardest part of facing the future is dealing with it when you don't want to. I charge you today to stop walking away from your issues, problems, and fears. You have to start facing them head on. Remember, you're not alone; Jesus is with you. His Word reminds us in Hebrews 13:5 that he will never leave us nor forsake us. Yes, this thing called purpose requires a lot from us: change in your thought process, how you view life, and more. Remember it's your destiny to live a purpose-filled life. It's the very reason you were created.

DAY 2

I prophesy uncommon favor over you this week in Jesus's name. Be strong today, be lifted, and stay in the grind. Think about the person that God has created—you. You're talented, beautiful, and way more gifted than you give your self credit for. Expect nothing less or more than what you put in! Today, give it all you've got! Galatians 6:7 (NIV) says, "Do not be deceived: God cannot be mocked. A man reaps what he sows." Don't allow situations that occur to shut your mouth or hinder you from doing what the Lord has purposed. Trials, haters, circumstances, and other obstacles will come, but you must stay the course and keep going.

Sometimes we move too quickly and forget to cover ourselves. Don't allow the enemy to creep through the back door. Make sure your house is locked tight. The enemy is always looking for a way in. Your day, your time, your month, and your year is here! For every second you've cried, for every seed you've sown, for all the time you thought you wasted, I am here to tell you that the Lord said that he has not forgotten about you. He has sent a package to you via priority Fed-Ex. Just don't allow the enemy, or your own voice to come in to put God in question on what he has spoken. This is not the time to rationalize or interrogate what he has said. Stand on it, decree and declare it!

We have to remind ourselves daily that it isn't about what we want or about what someone else wants but about what the Lord has already willed for us to have. People will express their opinions and even their logic behind what and why they believe you should or shouldn't proceed with your plans. But the Lord does not deal in logic or opinions. When the Lord tells you to go, stop, move forward, proceed with caution, pray, stand still, take off, or take any other action, you have to do it, or else you will miss what he has for you.

I encourage you to pursue and do what the Lord gifted you to do. You're going to do mighty works for the kingdom. It's okay; people make mistakes. Yes, several times we may think back on those mistakes and past failures, they can even become haunting and tormenting sometimes if we don't realize the power of freedom that we possess in Jesus Christ to overcome. Stand up when you fall, give God some praise, and get the ball rolling again. You have too much to do; you haven't even reached the tip of the icebergs yet. (Notice I said icebergs with an *s*.) Yes, multiple talents equal multiple businesses, purposes, and ministries but yet one destiny.

The Lord is adding and taking away. Our past has no business being connected to our future. Oh by way, all the trash has to go. ALL OF IT! It's time to fire some people.

We might not understand everything that happens, but we will most certainly learn from what happens. Know your worth. It will help you stand against people, habits, and issues that subtract from your life. Transparency is such a great quality and will help you win more people to the kingdom.

If you focus on one way of teaching, you will be stuck with

the same type of people. Don't shut out people because they don't agree with you or believe like you do. Pray and seek wisdom on how to approach them. The Lord's way works every time.

To understand who you are, you need to understand who you are not. Do you become frustrated when character traits show up, but you know the Lord has delivered you? You say to yourself, "I've been delivered of this. Why is it here?" Well, when you were delivered, the problem wasn't free from you, you were free from the problem. So it will always be there; you just have to make the godly choice not to give into it .

Emotions will surface, but you have to learn to keep them under control and in their right context. Your emotions can and will lie to you, keeping you upset and away from the world and the people that care. This is neither healthy for your mind or your spiritual maturity. Yes, this affects purpose!

In order to win, you sometimes have to lose. But are you really losing or just waiting for your turn? Yes, we all must wait in line for what God has for us, cutting in front of other people and trying to get ahead illegally only moves you to the back of the line. Rejoice—your turn is coming soon.

Today, do something you dread doing or something you've been procrastinating. Encourage someone you wouldn't normally call. Extend your hand to someone other than your friends or family.

It's time to step outside your circle. The Lord did not tell you to not associate with different groups of people. They may talk different, look different, dress different, of a different race, or culture…but that's kingdom!. The Lord is never clichish if that's a word.. Probably not, but you get my point. He never discounted those who were different. As a matter of fact, he actually brought us into an amazing promise! You made that choice because of how you felt. It's time to release those feelings. You never know if the person you been avoiding might be the one the Lord is sending to help and and encourage you to a place of purpose. Different don't always mean dangerous, sometimes it simply means ordained!

DAY 3

No one likes words of rebuke, and no one likes to hear the word forfeited. Although we might step out of the will of God at times and get off course, we are given an opportunity to jump back in and try it again. Life might seemingly be put on hold, and some things didn't work out like you had hoped. But you overcame, and now you are ready to get back in there and win. Psalm 37:23–24 (ESV) tells us, "The steps of a man are established by the Lord, when he delights in his way; though he fall he shall not be cast headlong, for the Lord upholds his hand." The Lord is releasing the next set of instructions. Get ready, for he is completing the vision.

All that you were doing before, everything that you were going through, and everything you had to fight through was just the precursor to what the Lord is getting ready to do now. Now the work begins.

Because of where you are headed, you will feel like you are going through practically every test in the book. Big test, little test, repeated test, someone else's test, hard test, easy test, flesh test, character test, faith test, marriage test, relationship test, money test, peace test, mind test, leadership test, people test. You name it; it is being thrown your way. But you must not throw in the towel! The Lord is enlarging and stretching you for greater.

Weaknesses. Yes. we will have them. Struggles. Yes, we will have them. Failures and falling short. Yes, they will happen. Let downs. Yes, they will happen. But try again. Try again. Try again! The worst decision you will ever make is to turn your back and walk away from purpose because of a person, mistake, issue, or problem. Yes, character counts in the success of pursuing purpose. If you have to lie, steal, fake it, cheat, or deceive to get it, more than likely, it's not for you. Turn away quickly, get back in there, and win.

Identity 101: God can't use what he did not place inside you.

Only what he placed in you will be effective for use in kingdom building.

Movement of your mouth, limbs, hands, feet, ideas, and what the Lord has placed inside you are connected to your survival. It cannot continue to stand still. Don't allow fear to paralyze you.

The Lord will cause change to come by simply letting you know that he loves you. Seven days of showing and displaying love has the ability to completely change the course of a person's life? Love is so powerful. It has the potency to erase and eradicate seven years of rejection and pain! Love changed me; let it change you too. I love you, sister or brother.

DAY 4

You just have to start. The Lord already completed the vision before he told you to do it. Psalms 32:8 (ESV) says, "I will instruct you and teach you in the way you should go; I will counsel you with my eye upon you." Habakkuk 2:2 (NKJV) tells us, "Then the Lord answered me and said, 'Write down the vision, and make it plain on tablets, that he may run who reads it.'" Step to the challenge, go face to face, and let the opposition know that it shall and will be defeated. Go ahead, look it square in the eyes and say, "You will not win. I have already overcome, and I am headed where I'm supposed to be. I will have what God said I will have, and I am who God says I am, in Jesus's name."

Give it a two piece with the Word and the Holy Spirit combined, followed by a knockout rebuke. Proceed with your daily duties, whether you're working, cleaning, going to school, running a business, or taking care of the kids. Be blessed. Realize what matters, and get rid of excess baggage. Release it. Time truly does reveal all things. Be patient and wait it out, and you will see great results. Faith without works is dead.

If the Lord showed you and told you, then know that he's made provision for you to do what he has said. Hint: If you have faith for little, you will receive little, but if you stretch your faith so that it's unlimited, you will receive an unlimited response. Think about it. Make plans to stand through the test. Speak it now. The miracle is in your mouth. Start commanding everything in your life to line up with the blessings of the Father in heaven in Jesus's name. Retaliation is never the answer. Christ has always been the perfect example of how to react in persecution. Disappointments will come, but stay focused on the real task at hand. Popularity doesn't mean anointed, or appointed. You are God's choice. His opinion is what truly matters. Stay focused. The Lord has already given it to you. Don't second guess yourself.

Circumstances will sometimes deceive you. Let's never be discouraged in the what we feel isn't happening or progressing forward. The Lord truly has a set time for everything. Wait and see. Get ready!

DAY 5

When changes are not coming fast enough and we need it to move now, we tend to make the biggest mistakes by reacting instead of waiting. Never allow pressure, panic, or too much anticipation to force you to make a decision that could potentially threaten, compromise, or cost you that million-dollar blessing that awaits ahead. Exodus 14:13 (KJV) tells us, "Stand still and see the salvation of the LORD." Psalm 27:14 (ESV) says, "Wait for the Lord; Be strong and let your heart take courage; Yes, wait for the LORD."

When one door closes, the Lord opens another door. Dry your eyes; the opportunity is coming again, and this time it's purposed for you. When you are trying to do the best that you can do and giving it your all—putting in long hours, making contacts, networking, praying, praising, declaring—and still nothing is happening, you must realize, that it has nothing to do with what you're doing. What you're trying to achieve was already done for you before you were born. You don't work for purpose; you walk into it.

The waiting game can be very exhausting. Waiting keeps the mind spinning in non-stop circles, so I have decided to stop the vicious cycle and take the batteries out of anything that has to do with what I'm believing the lord for. I will wait patiently for my turn.

Don't look at your failures as setbacks, but view them as tools to help you move forward. None of us has a perfect life, but the perfect sacrifice was given for all of us. And there may be a misjudgment or wrong choice or two involved…but it's okay, learn from it and keep going. It's just a stepping stool. Step up and step over it.

When you need to make decisions, pray and ask the Lord what to do. making wise choices will allow you to keep what you have with the ability to gain more. A foolish decision will always leave you with nothing. In this season of transition, seek the Lord before moving or taking the next step because, failing to do so this time around could cost you everything.

DAY 6

If it's causing you stress, let it go. It's not worth it to hold onto it where you are headed, and it's not worth totally giving up what you have been called to do. Try not to do so much at one time. Your focus and your ability to complete your purpose is more important than how many things you can do. The word for the weekend is rest and recover. Say it with me, "Rest and recover." Repeat it until it's in your spirit. You will need spiritual and natural strength to complete the next vision or assignment. You cannot operate with just one. Stay encouraged. Some great things are ahead of you—really! You need your strength to accomplish them.

Psalms 23:1-6 (NIV) tells us, "The LORD is my shepherd, I lack nothing. He makes me lie down in green pastures, he leads me beside quiet waters, he refreshes my soul. He guides me along the right paths for his name's sake. Even though I walk through the darkest valley, I will fear no evil, for you are with me; your rod and your staff, they comfort me. You prepare a table before me in the presence of my enemies. You anoint my head with oil; my cup overflows. Surely your goodness and love will follow me all the days of my life, and I will dwell in the house of the LORD forever."

"Do not be anxious about anything, but in every situation, by prayer and petition, with thanksgiving, present your requests to God. And the peace of God, which transcends all understanding, will guard your hearts and your minds in Christ Jesus." Philippians 4:6-7 (NIV). Ask yourself, Do I really believe and trust what the Lord say? Do I believe I can do it? Can I actually achieve it? The answer is…(Drum role) please… Yes you do and yes you can!

DAY 7

Change this one thing, and I promise you will move to the next level. Do not think that everyone is your enemy, hating you, praying against you, or chanting curses over you. Instead, believe that someone is thinking and praying about ways to bless you. He or she is at work, running a business, writing a book, coming up with the next million dollar idea, hosting a conference, attending school, tending to children, or shopping as you should be doing. We are what we think. Our mind can be our worst enemy if we let it. We are constantly thinking and reliving what people have done to us in our past, so we put that same label on everyone else. We might be suffering with inward insecurities, but we blame it on others. We automatically focus our anger and frustration toward those that appear to being doing better or those who seem to be against us when, in reality, their fruits show that they are for us. Be careful that you do not kick the wrong people to the curb. You could be kicking your blessing right out the door.

Philippians 4:8 (NIV) says, "Finally, brothers and sisters, whatever is true, whatever is noble, whatever is right, whatever is pure, whatever is lovely, whatever is admirable—if anything is excellent or praiseworthy—think about such things."

I have learned that whatever you believe or receive in your mind totally affects everything else. Today, I challenge you to think and believe only positive things. Pick out a few scriptures that apply to you and let them marinate in your mind and spirit. Shift your focus from people to purpose! Oh and apologize to those you may have offended and cast to the side based off the insecurities you were dealing with. I promise there is a major blessing waiting on the other end!

Matthew 5:23-24 "Therefore, if you are offering your gift at the alter and there remember that your brother or sister has something against you, leave your gift there in front of the altar. First go and be reconciled to that person. Then come and offer your gift.

DAY 8

You have to obey the Lord even when your own mind says that something looks right, seems right, smells right, and talks right. When the Lord says no, he means no.

Exodus 19:5 (NASB) admonishes us, "Now then, if you will indeed obey My voice and keep my covenant, then you shall be My own possession among all the peoples, for all the earth is Mine." Deuteronomy 28:1 (NIV) says, "If you fully obey the Lord your God and carefully follow all his commands I give you today, the Lord your God will set you high above all the nations on earth." I know that obedience sometimes sounds like a bad word or can even be seen as offensive if used in the wrong context. But the obedience that I am speaking of is the obedience that leads you to the blessing. Do whatever the Lord tells or instructs you to do. Don't continue to question it or not follow it because you feel like your way is best. If your way was best, your life would be incredible and amazing right now. When you choose to do it God's way, allow him to lead and guide you. I promise you that the reward will be amazing. Everything will turn out much better than you have ever dreamed. (See Ephesians 3:20-21.) Don't lose sight or becoming distracted with what everyone else is doing. What did God tell you to do? The spiritual meaning of the number 8 represents New Beginnings, but it cannot begin if you do not obey.

DAY 9

You won't miss a single thing. Expect, claim, and go get it. Philippians 4:19 (KJV) promises us, "But my God shall supply all your need according to his riches in glory by Christ Jesus."

Don't worry about missing out. Yes, you will have people—your leader, supervisor, parents, siblings, friends, and others—or even your own thoughts and insecurities that disagree with what the Lord is doing in your life. Just don't allow that to handicap what he has given you to do. Always do what you are asked, stay humble, and continue to pursue. Go after it, and stay the course. No you may not having an understanding of why this, or why that all the time, realistically, we are not supposed to. The main thing is staying the course. Certain things may happen in life, that may feel like a hurricane has swept through and disputed and dismantled everything. Whether you go to the doctor and receive a not so good report, you lose your job, have relationship issues, or marital problems; You cannot lose sight, you must continue to push forward.

DAY 10

Rise and shine today! Whatever is fighting you, let it go! The word is "It's coming to pass." It's been shifted in your favor. The Lord is doing some explosive things for the year! It's has already begun. Manifestations are already showing up. Don't be afraid to invest in yourself and the ideas that the Lord has given you to do! Never be afraid to invest in yourself because you feel like its's going to fail or because "everyone " else is doing it. The same amount of money that you invest in buying hair from different hair stores, clothes from different retailers and boutiques, products from the grocery store, book stores, makeup from different cosmetic lines, leasing and renting properties, paying someone to cut your lawn, or whatever you spend your own money on, is the same amount of money the Lord wants you to invest in what he has given you to do. You are the business owner, the property owner, the designer, the retailer, the author, the movie producer, the writer, the director, the health and fitness instructor, the stylist ect… Listen, you are the brand that everyone wants to buy! The Lord didn't stop blessing people with brands after all the major ones were created. The same amount of trust that you have when buying their products that it is going to work and do what you purchased it for is the same amount of trust I want you to have in people buying the product or idea that I have given to you. Where do you think the all the major ideas came from? If I can plant an idea in them and it prospers.. what about what I have planted in you?????

Touching and Agreeing with You

I am praying and touching and agreeing with you for whatever you are seeking the Lord to do. 1 Samuel 2:26 (ESV) tells us, "Now the boy Samuel was growing in stature and in favor both with the LORD and with men." Proverbs 12:2 (NASB) promises, "A good man will obtain favor from the Lord, but he will condemn a man who devises evil." Numbers 6:25 (NASB) says, "The LORD make his face shine on you, And be gracious to you."

DAY 11

Nothing is perfect, but everything we experience and go through in life works perfectly to bring us higher or to the next place in life. Be strong. Be encouraged. Today is yet another day for winning. Today my prayer for you is to complete what you started.

Let's Pray:

Father, in the name of Jesus, we know that it is your will for us to prosper spiritually and naturally. Your word in 3 John 1:2 (KJV) says, "Beloved, I wish above all things that thou mayest prosper and be in health, even as thy soul prospereth." Lord, give us the confidence to trust you in spite of what we see, hear, or encounter. As you continue to unravel who I am, who you have called me to be, and what you have called me to do, give me the patience to trust the process. Romans 8:28 (KJV) reminds us, "And we know that all things work together for good to them that love God, to them who are the called according to his purpose." In Jesus's name, Amen!

DAY 12

Trust the plan! Twelve is the biblical number for government. The Lord is lining everything up and putting them together. Geographic location, area, or state will mean nothing. The Lord is shifting the scene. Writers, authors, artists, actors, talk-show hosts, radio hosts, movie producers, directors, screenplay writers, singers, dancers, designers, hairstylists, makeup artists, and all types of creatives: Get ready for an explosive year! Hollywood is coming to you. Now is your word. You were blocked because of your beliefs and unwillingness to compromise, but now you have been released. Thus saith the Lord. And it is so in Jesus's name. Philippians 4:13 (KJV) promises, "I can do all things through Christ which strengtheneth me." Proverbs 16:3 (NIV) says, "Commit to the Lord whatever you do, and he will establish your plans." 1 Kings 2:3 (NIV) tells us, "And observes what the Lord your God requires: walk in obedience to him, and keep his decrees and commands, his laws and regulations, as written in the law of Moses. Do this so that you may prosper in all you do and wherever you are."

DAY 13

Don't doubt the promise. When I say that the Lord is amazing, he is amazing, and he wants to bless you. James 1:6 (NIV) says, "But when you ask, you must believe and not doubt, because the one who doubts is like a wave of the sea, blown and tossed by the wind." If you are in the birthing process, remember this. Transition is uncomfortable, irritating, aggravating, emotional, highly frustrating, and exhausting. But you must remain in a place of peace and of being still. I know it's hard, especially if you are preparing to give birth to multiples. You are suffering twice and three times as much because of the magnitude of what you are carrying. But you must endure in order to birth what God has for you. Don't abort your dream because of the labor pains. It's all part of the process. Continue to be encouraged.

Release and let go of what makes your mind heavy. Sometimes you can overthink a situation so that it eventually turns from a thought into full-blown stress.

Take charge of what the Lord has given you. Nothing will move, change, or happen unless you take the first step. You can be afraid of the unknown, but don't allow fear to hold you back.

Let's Pray:

Father, in the name of Jesus,

Give me the strength to stay the course although old habits old feelings, past hurts, and past rejections might try to arise. Renew my mind and heart. Let a fresh wind blow upon me, giving me your outlook and your perception. I know that fear is only an attempt to keep me from moving forward and a detour from the path of success. Today I give fear no more power, but I renounce it now. I will not be afraid of a no because, where there is a closed door, Lord, you have an open one. For your Word says in Psalms 118:6 (NIV), "The LORD is with me; I will not be afraid. What can mere mortals do to me?"

In the name of Jesus, I step forth and decree that I shall live and not die. I shall go forth in what you have called me to do without fear or shame. I shall not feel defeated because I have victory. In Jesus's name, Amen.

DAY 14

Today let's focus on what's to come and not what has been. You might have experienced the empty promises of opportunity or someone promising that they would do this or that for you, but it never happened. Yes, it hurt you and brought you a lot of disappointment, leaving a sour taste in your mouth. But you recovered and gave it to the Lord, which released favor to act on your behalf. The tables just turned. The Lord just moved you into a place where people will no longer just speak empty promises to you, such as "I'm praying for you." They will no longer just pat you on the back, but they will build, support, finance, produce, press in, pour in, push, promote, assist, and help you to where you are going.

DAY 15

You have been shifted overnight into a different place. God will provide today. You have been restored, confirmed, strengthened, and established. Everything unproductive in your life has just been fired. Your reach has been extended. Today you must revisit the vision board. Continue to remind yourself of what the Lord has spoken to you. Continue to pray and seek him concerning the next set of instructions. I know it can become frustrating while you are waiting, but you are no longer in the same place. Your continuous yes has shifted somethings in your life. Stay with the plan, and trust the Lord.

DAY 16

One of the most amazing truths is that Jesus still lives. And because he lives, you can also live. Continue to trust his promises for your life. Discouragements will happen, and things might not always seems like they are changing or moving fast enough, but it's okay; the Lord is with you. He will never leave you or forsake you. Stress has no place in your life because you have a promise. Where there is a promise, there is life.

1 Kings 8:56 (NASB) reminds us, "Blessed be the LORD, who has given rest to His people Israel, according to all that He promised; not one word has failed of all His good promise, which He promised through Moses His servant."

Genesis 28:15 (ESV) says, "Behold, I am with you and will keep you wherever you go, and will bring you back to this land; for I will not leave you until I have done what I have promised you."

1 Corinthians 15:20 (KJV) tells us, "But now is Christ risen from the dead, and become the firstfruits of them that slept."

1 John 5:13 (KJV) says, "These things have I written unto you that believe on the name of the Son of God; that ye may know that ye have eternal life, and that ye may believe on the name of the Son of God."

John 3:16 (KJV) promises, "For God so loved the world that he gave his only begotten Son, that whosoever believeth in him should not perish, but have everlasting life."

DAY 17

A door cannot close if you never tried to open it. Some doors have been unlocked and open, waiting on you to turn the handle and walk through. You are the key. What the Lord has placed in you is about to become the answer to unlocking opportunities for the next generation of talent, business owners, and entrepreneurs.

Lord, I pray that you reveal the next step. Show your people which decision to make and which way to turn today. Lord, being at a crossroads isn't easy. Your people don't want to move without you, ahead of you, or procrastinate. We want what you want for our lives. If the answer is no, we will stay put and continue to work the vision from where we are. If it's go and pursue, then we will pursue. If it's wait, then we will wait until it's time. Give us wisdom as to which house to choose, which business to open, which job to take, what story to write, which church to join, what ministry to start, what conference to attend or to host, what bank to ask for the grant, who to connect with, who to collaborate with, who to marry, who to talk to, who to let go of, and who to keep. Just don't let your people make any more decisions without you! It's just too crucial to the call and purpose on our lives in this season.

Psalms 25:4-5 (KJV) tells us, "Shew me thy ways, O Lord; teach me thy paths. Lead me in thy truth, and teach me; for thou art the God of my salvation; on thee do I wait all the day."

DAY 18

If you only partially submit to the Lord and hold onto inward doubt, you will not manifest what he has spoken concerning your life. Yes, it can be tough to obey and submit to the plan of God, especially if the plan seems overwhelming and impossible to accomplish. Sometimes it might even feel like we bit off more than we could chew. But all in all, if we could not accomplish it, it wouldn't exist. Today, doubt has to be eradicated and put out of its misery so that you are able to move forward with the tenacity and fervor that you once had.

Joshua 1:7 (ESV) tells us, "Only be strong and very courageous, being careful to do according to all the law which Moses my servant commanded you. Do not turn from it to the right hand or to the left, that you may have success wherever you go."

Psalm 42:11 (NASB) says, "Why are you in despair, O my soul? And why have you become disturbed within me? Hope in God, for I shall yet praise Him, The help of my countenance and my God."

Psalm 40:8 (NASB) tells us, "I delight to do Your will, O my God; Your Law is within my heart." Hebrews 13:21 (NASB) says, "equip you in every good thing to do His will, working in us that which is pleasing in His sight, through Jesus Christ, to whom be the glory forever and ever. Amen."

Be encouraged today, my brother or sister. The issues and problems and what you might struggle with day to day will never agree or confirm where you are headed... but they will most certainly push you in the right direction. Acts 7:9 (KJV) reminds us, "And the patriarchs, moved with envy, sold Joseph into Egypt: but God was with him."

Genesis 39:21 (KJV) says, "But the LORD was with Joseph, and shewed him mercy, and gave him favour in the sight of the keeper of the prison."

DAY 19

My sister or my brother, you're being molded for something far greater. Good news: The Lord said that you can let go now; he has this. The same miracle the Lord allowed you to walk through will be the same one he uses to help someone else run through theirs.

What you saw was amazing. It wasn't you. It wasn't your imagination or just a good thought. The lord divinely interrupted your life to show you what he has for you. Yes, he spoke it. He showed it, and now he's going to perform it. The right word applied in the wrong season could be devastating. Stop and seek the Lord for his timing. Too early, too soon, too late, and behind schedule is not good enough. Purpose needs you on time. Brother, sister, there comes a time when the word becomes silent, and you just simply miss out. God wasn't off. The word wasn't off. The pastor wasn't off. The prophet wasn't off. The dream you had wasn't off. You just didn't move. Joshua 23:14 (NASB) promises, "Now behold, today I am going the way of all the earth, and you know in all your hearts and in all your souls that not one word of all the good words which the LORD your God spoke concerning you has failed; all have been fulfilled for you, not one of them has failed."

DAY 20

The enemy wants to stop it before it prospers.. He wants to kill it before it leaves this year. He wants to shut it down before it flourishes into the vision God has ordained it to be in the coming year. Although the enemy is fighting the vision, he cannot stop it. Although he is sending people to disrupt the vision, he cannot divide the vision. Although he has sent arrows and darts of negativity toward your vision, it will not hinder the vision. The vision shall go on and it shall prosper. John 10:10 (NIV) promises "The thief comes only to steal and kill and destroy; I have come that they may have life, and have it to the full." Even more important than your name is your influence. When the enemy discovers that he can't kill you, he will pursue you to kill your reputation. Rejoice, for your greater is ahead, but your past is behind you.

Unlink with people who have already decided and predetermined how far you can be blessed. Before you end the night, the Lord told me to tell you the reason why it happened was because you needed to walk alone for a season with no distractions, no interruptions, no persuasions, no opinions, no opposers, and no negative influences. All you needed was him and the word he spoke to you. Get ready for the bigger, for the kingdom of God has no limits.

Today I am praying that the Lord will send you relationships, connections, people, friends, and family who aren't jealous, trying to copy, trying to outdo, secretly in competition, questioning, opposing, lying, or sabotaging the anointing or calling on your life. I'm praying instead that he will send those that will love you, embrace you, lift you up in prayer, help you, counsel you, encourage you, support you, and speak those hard truths to you that you need to hear. If they always agree with you, something is wrong. We are not always right, and if they agree with what is wrong, then you have problem. I know that similar types of people seem to show up in your life. They have a different face but the same spirit. Today that breaks. I know that you have a good heart, and you want to help everyone. But you have to use godly discernment about who you link up with, especially in this season of your life. Everybody isn't for you. Listen, it's all right. The Lord is changing your circle. Don't fight it. Embrace it. Be encouraged. Deuteronomy 31:8 (NASB) tells us, "The LORD is the one who goes ahead of you; He will be with you. He will not fail you or forsake you. Do not fear or be dismayed."

DAY 21

There is nothing more beautiful than the ability to forgive.

1 John 1:9 (GNT) says, "But if we confess our sins to God, he will keep his promise and do what is right: he will forgive us our sins and purify us from all our wrongdoing."

Ephesians 4:31-32 (GNT) reminds us, "Get rid of all bitterness, passion, and anger. No more shouting or insults, no more hateful feelings of any sort. Instead, be kind and tender-hearted to one another, and forgive one another, as God has forgiven you through Christ."

No, they might have done you wrong in the past, they might have overlooked over you, treated you indifferently, and maybe even lied about you. But those things are in the past. Even if it happened yesterday or a minute ago, time is still moving and ticking. Every second you waste on thinking about what someone has done can keep you from moving forward. Never give a person so much power over your destiny that they could ultimately ruin it.

Let's Pray:

Father, in the name of Jesus,

I forgive, and I let go of all the bitterness and anguish I feel toward that person. Regardless of what they might have done, he or she is not worth losing my purpose and what you have called me to do. Father, it's hurts within, and sometimes I want to say and do things I shouldn't, but I am reminded of your promise in 2 Corinthians 12:9a (NIV). "But he said to me, 'My grace is sufficient for you, for my power is made perfect in weakness.'"

You are made stronger in my weaknesses. Be the strength that I need to love regardless of the offense. Father, forgive me for not forgiving them. Hurt people hurt people, and I need you to heal me every place it hurts so that I won't hurt anyone else. I want to move on and not be hindered and stuck where I am because of un-forgiveness. Lord, I let it go now, in Jesus's name!

DAY 22

The Lord shifts the meaning of the word different to mean anointed. Don't blend in but accept and embrace your differences because the Lord is getting ready to use them. Jeremiah 1:7-8 (NIV) says, "But the Lord said to me, 'Do not say, "I am too young." You must go to everyone I send you to and say whatever I command you. Do not be afraid of them, for I am with you and will rescue you,' declares the Lord."

Your DNA makeup or your creativity might not look like others. But that's okay; you have been created to stand out so that you can be more effective when it's time to bring it in. Don't ever become discouraged because you don't sound, look, or act like them. You have been created as unique so that you can be effective in the purpose that God has called you to. Embrace your differences; they look great on you.

DAY 23

The Lord wanted me to encourage you and let you know that the amount of spiritual warfare you have been experiencing is the amount of blessings you are about to receive as you enter the new year. Be encouraged because God sees and knows. Good news: The Lord just picked you to be next. It will get hard sometimes, and everything around you will seem impossible to conquer. You might suffer loss of friends, loss of relationships, and loss of finances, but you can still be victorious. Resist the urge to quit. Elevation comes with separation. You are in a new season.

Callings don't come after the story. The story reveals the process and purpose of the call. The test brings out how you feel and what's in you, what is coming out of you. Maybe this is the time to just let it all out because once it's gone, you can move onto the next task.

DAY 24

Do you have faith or just a stubborn will? Don't allow how you perceive what you are going through to kill your belief in what the Lord has spoken. The Lord is watching over his word to perform it. Sometimes we pursue after or hold on to something that was never meant for us to have and call it faith. But we are sadly disappointed when it doesn't come to pass. The best place to be is in the will of God. I just wanted to encourage you today to know the will of God for your life. It will never fail you. Colossians 1:9 (ESV) reminds us, "For this reason also, since the day we heard of it, we have not ceased to pray for you and to ask that you may be filled with the knowledge of His will in all spiritual wisdom and understanding."

Jeremiah 1:12 (NIV) says, "The LORD said to me, 'You have seen correctly, for I am watching to see that my word is fulfilled.'"

DAY 25

Heaven is experiencing an unusual high call volume. Your estimated wait time is no more than what the Lord is allowing. Hold and remain on the line. Your prayers will be answered shortly!

The main key to your destiny is making the right decision. I know you have some things pulling and tugging at you. But today, I am touching and agreeing with you that the Lord sends direction and confirmation of what to do! You can't make a decision based on emotions or on your present circumstances. Make the right decision according to his plan and what he has willed for you to do. You have a part that he's given you in the piece of the puzzle. This is what needs to happen in order to ensure a successful outcome.

Spiritual surgery doesn't always feel good, especially when you are not prepared or when the pain is not numbed before the operation. If you are numb, you might not detect or realize you have an issue in a certain area. Sometimes the immediate removal or the cutting away of whatever it is, is necessary before it spreads and kills your hope, your, purpose, what the Lord has placed inside of you, and ultimately your destiny.

You must be who God called you to be. The ministry the Lord has given you is uniquely diverse. With every trial and test that you are and have overcome, he is expanding you to handle the greatness of it. This ministry is catered to reach millions at a time. He said I am and have been delivering you from people so that you can walk without fear of their faces or of their words. You will go in areas others cannot go. You will travel lands that others are forbidden to go to because of their inability to be open to the will and heart of God. So don't draw back, shut your mouth, go into a cave, be quiet, or conform to someone else's identity or opinion of who or what you should be or what you should be doing. What did the Lord say? What does his word say? Stay with that, and you will forever win.

You will survive. Trust in the Lord's plan for your life. He allows some of things to happen to bring out the best in you. At times, he wants to show you what's in you or around you that's holding you back.

DAY 26

Your pocketbook does not dictate your future, but it can change it if you don't sow to the right source. invest into the kingdom

Allow truth to stand up in your life. If you have to lie about it, then you shouldn't say it. God always defends truth, but a lie will always fail.

Forget about what happened the last time you tried to be honest. This time around, it will work.

What is life if you aren't happy? If you are always upset, down, depressed, and unhappy in the relationship you're in, whether it's a friendship or relationship, you probably need to evaluate it further and possibly just let it go. Peace of mind and in the mind is everything . Pray again and see what the Lord says.

The Lord told me to tell you this morning to keep an open mind. Don't discount your decision one way or the other. He said he is blessing both ways. The contract, the grant, the idea, and or the proposal is already destined to be approved so that the vision springs forth, starting this year. It wobbled off the ground some years back. You saw it grow a little, but it still did not work the way the Lord showed you nor did the finances come the way you expected. But get ready, brother or sister, your idea is about to be picked up. And it is so in Jesus's name.

DAY 27

The one thing people fear the most is being alone. Some of us have been in constant relationships, one after the other, person after person, whether long-term relationships, one-night stands, or just nightly hook ups. Or even just putting yourself out there to be used for the sake of having someone near you. For one reason or another, we have allowed the fear of being alone to make choices for us. Know that you are never alone and that the Lord is always with you!! Stop allowing people to abuse your time when the Lord has already set it aside for himself.

The challenges we face will often seem unbearable, especially those that say, "I'm right, and you're wrong." In this case, who's listening to who? Winning is not always the key. but resolving the problem unlocks doors that have been closed for years. The enemy will always try and place what you used to struggle with in front of your face. You might sometimes even feel like you have never been saved and that your change was only temporary. Each time, the fight is even greater than before. Just remember as you go higher in the Lord, you will face higher levels of demons, higher levels of trials, and higher levels of attacks. But when all is said and done, the things we face produce a high level of anointing with the added bonus of a high priority blessing sent directly to you.

Congratulations! You dodged a bullet. At one time, you felt left out and left behind, only to find out that the Lord was shielding you from contamination, a tainted walk, and the old religious way of thinking. You were never meant to connect with those who sweep it under the rug, keep it a secret, hush it up, or hide the truth. You were never meant to hook up with, share a stage with, work with, travel with, minister with, or make money with them. Those alliances would have cost you everything. Instead, it's time for out with the old and in with the new. Get ready, your set time has arrived.

The situation blew your mind when it happened, and you

almost gave up. The problem tried to set you back, confuse you, cause you to question, cause you to doubt, and cause you to go back to the same ole same ole. But God! I hear the Lord saying that this was only to provoke you to greater: greater power, greater anointing, greater glory, greater doors, greater trust, greater ambition, greater ideas—greater, *greater*, ***greater***!

The yes that you gave to the Lord yesterday provoked a turnaround while you were asleep last night. It's been approved. Reapply, rewrite, resubmit, redo, go back, and get it!

What are you worried about? This will happen as planned. It will work out, sound right, look right, and go right.

Don't allow your situation to speak to you. Instead, turn around and speak to the situation. Aren't you tired of being bullied, pushed over, dog walked, pimped, put down, and told what to do by your circumstances? If so, start standing and commanding. Stop putting off for tomorrow what can be accomplished today. Sometimes tomorrow turns into next week and then next month and into years. Don't delay in what the Lord has given you to do as it will hold up your purpose. Don't worry about what they say you can't have, but rejoice over what the Lord said. He promised that it's yours.

The people who excluded you on purpose didn't know that they were helping to set you up for greater than what they have, exceedingly above the same thing that they tried to keep you from.

The Lord told me to tell you this morning that you can now be trusted to catapult to the next level. Get ready. Promotion is here.

When you know your life requires the presence of God and your survival in this race depends on it, your consistency in worship will put a demand on the anointing.

The reason you never give up is because God never gave up.

Because he lives, you can live too. While life is tough and sometimes appears a little less promising than we hope, we have a promise of victory. We can keep pushing and press past any and all obstacles that try to block our way. Keep going. The best is yet to come.

DAY 28

No matter if you have many gifts and talents or think that you have only one, the following is for you. You have brainstormed enough, went back and forth, and shuffled through ideas. You thought it was this, but now it's that. You want to do a hundred different things, sometimes all at once. The Lord said that if you are stretched too many different ways, you will not fulfill your intended purpose. If you focus on building the one thing, he said that he will cause the one to finance and open the doors for the rest!

Matthew 25:15-23 (ESV) says in the parable of the talents that "To one he gave five talents, to another two, to another one, to each according to his ability. Then he went away. He who had received the five talents went at once and traded with them, and he made five talents more. So also he who had the two talents made two talents more. But he who had received the one talent went and dug in the ground and hid his master's money. Now after a long time the master of those servants came and settled accounts with them. And he who had received the five talents came forward, bringing five talents more, saying, 'Master, you delivered to me five talents; here, I have made five talents more.' His master said to him, 'Well done, good and faithful servant. You have been faithful over a little; I will set you over much. Enter into the joy of your master.' And he also who had the two talents came forward, saying, 'Master, you delivered to me two talents; here, I have made two talents more.' His master said to him, 'Well done, good and faithful servant. You have been faithful over a little; I will set you over much."

DAY 29

You are uncomfortable where you are because the timing of God is now calling forth what he has placed in you to be released. Let's be intentional today about pursuing purpose! The Lord said to stop wondering where it's going to come from. He is using what's in your house to bring you wealth. You are the answer. Your ideas, your hands, your ability to create, speak, design, build, write, coordinate, plan, solve problems, and help others with theirs. Wow, that's eleven streams already. Do not delay any longer. I have the feeling that today will be a good day.

Listen, association does not automatically qualify a person for favor, God does. If you are a business owner or if you desire to be a business owner, designer, have a service company, or you use your gift to help the community in any type of way, divine favor is about to meet you right where you are!

Purposed pain is the discomfort of the trial that pushes you closer to the Lord. Continue to seek him. It's about ministry this time.

Listen, a single wrong thought can dismantle the will of God for your life if you allow it to. Be careful of thoughts that oppose your purpose. Cast them down and keep moving. That was last year's trial. Your season for being bound in the mind is over. Let it go, and let God do the rest.

People often judge you by what they see. Listen, pictures capture moments of a person's life, not their entire stories. #Beware of being discouraged by false narratives that look like something they are not.

Listen, those other people or things only work if you give them power. Rebuke them in Jesus's name and keep moving. Just because God is blessing, shifting, and changing the season doesn't mean the irritation and the provoking of the enemy goes away. As a matter of fact, it goes to another level, so you must continue to fight, press, and pray even while you're being blessed. Continue to be encouraged.

If we knew everything that we would have to face and go through to achieve certain goals or to obtain the promises the

Lord has ordained for us, we probably would have given up a long time ago. The Lord knows that we become pretty discouraged when the situation looks bleak. But the Lord loves us so much that he continues to show and gives us a constant reminder of what he has willed and purposed for our lives.

The reason you feel the way you feel is because you stop believing in your heart in the plan that I set for you. Yes, you go through the motions, but I read the heart. Come back into my grace, and I will soon show you the power of my joy. If you have stopped believing in the vision because of the trials and hardships that you face, I declare the same word over your life that the Lord gave me today. It's time to get your strength back. It's time to stand and prevail against the plan of the enemy. Get into the grace of God, and get your life back, in Jesus's name.

I know it seems like the Lord isn't with you. Lately it seems harder than ever to get a breakthrough. I want to encourage you as I encourage myself. Don't give up. He hears you. He loves you. He will never forsake you. And he is always with you.

Sometimes, you feel like you're right back where you started only to find out that you're only a moment away from your blessing. Stay in the race.

One of the most common mistakes is thinking that you can do it on your own. Yes, we all know that you are a big girl or a big boy, but maturity admits that you still need help although you are an adult. As long as the Lord showed you and told you, that's all that matters. Don't allow others looking at your situation to dictate what you need to do. You should listen to good advice, but it's even better to listen to the direction of God's voice.

We must live; existing is just not good enough. Anyone can exist, but the Lord offers a life of living in love, joy, peace, hope, and freedom.

Hebrews 12:1 (ESV) tells us, "Therefore, since we are

surrounded by so great a cloud of witnesses, let us also lay aside every weight, and sin which clings so closely, and let us run with endurance the race that is set before us."

Galatians 5:7-8 (ESV) says, "You were running well. Who hindered you from obeying the truth? That kind of persuasion does not come from the one who calls you."

Psalm 16:11 (ESV) states, "You make known to me the path of life; in your presence there is fullness of joy; at your right hand are pleasures forevermore."

DAY 30

We cannot control the wind whenever it blows. It can mess up your hair, blow your clothing, or even cause you to shiver a bit. The wind is a constant reminder that God is in control.

Psalm 78:26 (NASB) states, "He caused the east wind to blow in the heavens And by His power He directed the south wind." Amos 4:13 (NASB) says, "For behold, He who forms mountains and creates the wind And declares to man what are His thoughts, He who makes dawn into darkness And treads on the high places of the earth, The LORD God of hosts is His name."

Hey, my sister or brother: the trial you are in or just came out of is all about to make sense. The Lord is revealing another piece of the puzzle. Get somewhere quiet today just a few minutes. I don't care where you are: , work, home, church, school, in the airport, or outside. The Lord will allow you to see it, know it, and go forth in it to obtain it. God bless you today. Continue to be encouraged.

Listen, we can't afford to play Russian roulette with our purpose. The enemy is playing for keeps. We have to continue to open our mouths and command every situation to align. We have to command our minds to come under subjection and command our flesh to submit to the word of God. Yes, temptations will come; tests and trials will come, but we have the power to overcome them all through Jesus Christ who strengthens us. Continue to be encouraged.

There will always be opposition toward and against the call and the anointing that God has placed on your life. Just stay focused. Some opposition was sent to simply elevate you to the next place. Remember, even your haters have an assignment. And it's called talk him or her into their blessing. Listen, because somebody talked, you were just blessed. Keep going. Please don't stop pursuing your dreams. Your purpose is counting on you. We are counting on you. I know it's tempting to go back, stop, do something else, go somewhere else, or just drop it all together. But you must push past it. It's okay. Today is a new day. Get back up and try again. The devil is a liar. You can do it, and you will have victory over it. Giving up is not an option. You have been in this place before. I know everything seems still right now, and circumstances aren't going the way you hoped. But I promise that if you just hold on and keep going, the reward will be amazing. Continue to work the vision. Come on sis . . . come on bro . . . you're almost to the finish line. The Lord is doing some amazing things in this season and he's starting with you.

Notes:

Notes:

Notes:

Notes:

Notes:

Notes:

Notes:

Notes:

Notes:

Notes:

Notes:

Notes:

Notes:

Notes:

Notes:

Printed in Great Britain
by Amazon

31331049R00059